35 Coconut Fl[

The Delicious Gluten-Free, Paleo Alternative to Wheat

by

Anita Thomas

DISCLAIMER

Hello and welcome to *35 Coconut Flour Recipes: The Delicious Gluten Free, Paleo Alternative to Wheat.*

This book is all about delivering tasty alternatives to your favorite wheat based dishes. Many people suffer with gluten allergies and it's estimated that approximately 83% of Americans suffer with or are undiagnosed with celiac disease, an autoimmune condition where the villi in the small intestine is damaged, interfering with the absorption of nutrients.

A celiac diet, otherwise known as gluten-free is recommended for recovery because it removes all gluten that's found in grains like wheat, barley and rye. This doesn't mean you have to miss out on your favorite dishes though, many of which may contain grains in the baking process.

Coconut flour is an excellent grain-free alternative to refined flours, meaning that you can enjoy plenty of baked foods without worrying about what's in it or having the unpleasant experience of an allergic reaction.

Inside the next few pages of this book, you will come across 35 of my favorite recipes that use coconut flour in place of traditional baking flours. When you try and make these, you may notice that the taste of coconut flour is slightly different from grain flours – yes, coconut flour does taste like coconut, but it's *not* overwhelming. Many people state it is mild in taste and you may be pleasantly surprised by how quickly you become accustomed to this new flavor.

For ease of reference I have split this book into five different sections, Breakfast, Breads, Lunches, Dinners and Desserts. Feel free to dip in and out of this recipe book at will, or use it as a reference guide for planning gluten-free breads, snacks, meals and special treats for the whole family.

Alongside the more traditional breads you'll find inside this book that there are muffins and cookie recipes, delicious cakes and sumptuous pies that when made at home will taste fresh, and be 100% completely gluten-free, without having to compromise on taste. Many of these recipes can be adapted to fit in with a paleo lifestyle too.

What's more you don't have to follow a gluten free lifestyle to enjoy these recipes – but you may like it so much more knowing the various benefits it can bring to your overall health!

To living a gluten free lifestyle,

Anita Thomas

Table of Contents

Breakfasts

Paleo Cereal

A delicious cereal made with chopped nuts, flax seeds and honey, this is best reserved for special treats rather than every day breakfast cereals.

Ingredients

¼ cup coconut flour
1/3 cup flax seeds
A cup of chopped nuts
A handful of sliced almonds
A cup of coconut flakes/chips
A handful of raisins and dried cranberries
1/8 cup pure cocoa powder
A sprinkle of cinnamon
1 tablespoon coconut oil
1 tablespoon maple syrup
1 teaspoon honey

Method

1. Blend all of the above ingredients into a mixer. Drizzle in a tablespoon of melted coconut oil, tablespoon of maple syrup and teaspoon of honey until the mixture becomes wet and clumpy.
2. Onto a baking sheet, place the mixture and bake in the oven for 20 minutes at 350 degrees. Once baked, take out of the oven and leave to cool off, before crunching the cereal up in your hand.

3. If the cereal is too thick, then leave it in the oven to cook for a while longer, before breaking it into chunk sized pieces.

Serves: 4-6

Nutritional Information:

Calories (Total): 2877kcal 131%. Carbohydrates: 152g 55%. Protein: 94g 86%. Fat: 205g 280%. Saturated Fat: 59g 243%. Cholesterol: 0mg 0%. Sodium: 65mg 4% Fiber: 71g 282%. Sugar: 62g 112%. Vitamin A: 6.8IU 0%. Vitamin C: 1.4mg 2%. Calcium: 278mg 28%. Iron: 11mg 61%. Potassium: 945mg 20%.

Coconut Flour Pancakes

A gluten-free alternative to traditional pancakes – these are low calorie and taste just as delicious as their wheat alternatives.

Ingredients

½ cup coconut four (more if needed to thicken)
1 teaspoon of baking soda
5 eggs
1 cup of homemade apple sauce (store bought works well too)
¼ cup butter or coconut oil
1 teaspoon vanilla (optional)
2 tablespoons of honey (optional)
¼ cup butter or coconut oil
Cinnamon to taste (optional)
Fruit such as bananas or berries (optional)

Method

1. Heat a large pancake griddle or a skillet.
2. Mix all of the above ingredients except for any optional items into a blender, whisking and then leaving to sit for 5 minutes until it thickens.
3. Add in bananas, berries or any optional extras and mix by hand.
4. Grease the skillet or the griddle with some butter or coconut oil.
5. Take a ¼ cup measure and spoon the pancakes onto the cooking surface.
6. Cook each side for 2-3 minutes until it starts bubbling and becomes easy to flip. Coconut flour pancakes can take a little longer than the traditional pancakes, so don't rush this process.
7. Top with some butter or any other items. Enjoy!

Serves: 4

Nutritional Information:

Calories (Total): 1082kcal 49%. Carbohydrates: 50g 18%. Protein: 32g 29%. Fat: 83g 113%. Saturated Fat: 47g 191%. Cholesterol: 1067mg 356%. Sodium: 1140mg 76%. 4% Fiber: 1.1g 4%. Sugar: 49g 89%. Vitamin A: 2944IU 59%. Vitamin C: 1.4mg 2%. Calcium: 158mg 16%. Iron: 4.6mg 26%. Potassium: 458mg 10%.

This oatmeal is super easy to make and tastes a bit like apple pie. It also has the added benefit of being gluten, sugar and grain free…

Ingredients

1 medium apple
1 cup water
¼ cup coconut flour
½ to ¾ teaspoons cinnamon
A tiny pinch of nutmeg
A tiny pinch of salt
2 packages of Stevia

Method

1. Peel the apple, remove the core and slice the apple lengthwise and then into thirds.
2. Mix the coconut flour, cinnamon, nutmeg, salt and Stevia into a large cereal bowl and then microwave for 3 minutes.
3. Serve and enjoy.

Serves: 1

Nutritional Information:

Calories (Total): 146kcal 7%. Carbohydrates: 32g 11%. Protein: 2.2g 2%. Fat: 1.5g 2%. Saturated Fat: 0.5g 2%. Cholesterol: 0mg 0%. Sodium: 30mg 2%. Fiber: 11.1g 44%. Sugar: 18g 33%. Vitamin A: 107IU 2%. Vitamin C: 12mg 16%. Calcium:43mg 4%. Iron: 0.6mg 3%. Potassium: 10mg 0%.

These pancakes are delicious on their own, or served with peanut butter or whipped cream. They taste the same as regular pancakes, except they feel 'lighter'.

Ingredients

5 eggs, separated
1/3 cup milk
2 tablespoons honey, melted if necessary
5 tablespoons butter, melted
½ teaspoon salt
1 teaspoon vanilla extract
1/3 cup coconut flour
½ teaspoon baking powder
1 tablespoon unsweetened cocoa powder
¼ cup chocolate chips, plus more for topping
Coconut oil

Method

1. Separate the egg yolks from the whites, beating the egg whites until soft peaks begin to form. Fold in and beat with the egg yolks and then add the milk, butter, vanilla, honey and the salt. Whisk in the cocoa powder, baking powder and the coconut flour. Then stir in the chocolate chips.
2. Into a pan heat a tablespoon of coconut oil. Spoon about ¼ of a cup of the batter into the pan. Allow this to cook for around 3 minutes or so before carefully flipping the pancake over. Allow this to cook for another 2-3 minutes on the other side until it's well cooked through. Then repeat this process with the remaining batter.
3. Serve with toppings like maple syrup, peanut butter and whipped cream. Then top with chocolate chips.

Serves: 4 – makes about 9 pancakes

Nutritional Information:

Calories (Total): 1639kcal 74%. Carbohydrates: 104g 38%. Protein: 50g 46%. Fat: 109g 149%. Saturated Fat: 53g 217%. Cholesterol: 1002mg 334%. Sodium: 1636mg 109%. Fiber: 30g 119%. Sugar: 59g 107%. Vitamin A: 3536IU 71%. Vitamin C: 0.8mg 1%. Calcium: 412mg 41%. Iron: 5.7mg 32%. Potassium: 587mg 12%.

Gluten Free Coconut Flour Waffles

These simple to prepare coconut flour waffles taste delicious, can be made in matter of minutes and freeze well too.

Ingredients
½ cup coconut flour
12 eggs
8 tablespoons butter, melted
4 tablespoons applesauce
4 tablespoons honey,
½ teaspoon salt

Method

1. Preheat the waffle irons onto a high heat, greasing the iron well.
2. Mix in all of the above ingredients into a bowl until it forms a smooth batter. Spread the batter evenly so that it covers all of the waffle irons.
3. Cook for 3 minutes. Then serve!

Serves: 3-4 waffles

Nutritional Information:

Calories (Total): 2808kcal 128%. Carbohydrates: 152g 55%. Protein: 99g 90%. Fat: 194g 265%. Saturated Fat: 89g 366%. Cholesterol: 2272mg 757%. Sodium: 3737mg 249%. Fiber: 42g 167%. Sugar: 90g 164%. Vitamin A: 6689IU 134%. Vitamin C: 1.9mg 3%. Calcium: 552mg 55%. Iron: 9.2mg 51%. Potassium: 1082mg 23%.

Gluten-Free Crepes

An easy to prepare gluten-free crepe that melts in the mouth. Prepare in batches and add honey, maple syrup, sugar, lemon juice or chocolate sauce to sweeten. Alternatively, add some cheese, vegetables or meats to create a savory version.

Instructions

2 cups coconut (or rice) flour
2 cups milk
2 eggs
¼ cup olive oil (1/2 tablespoon for each crepe)

Method

1. Into a bowl mix the coconut or rice flour, milk and eggs, using a fork to beat until smooth.
2. Heat a non-stick pan and then pour in ½ tbsp. oil.
3. Once the oil is very hot, a ladle of batter should be poured onto the same point in the pan. Roll the pan from side to side to give the batter a round shape.
4. Cook the batter for 1-2 minutes, checking the bottom with a spatula. Release the pancake and flip it once it's a light golden brown color.
5. Flip the pancake up and cook on the other side for 1-2 minutes, before transferring onto a plate.
6. Repeat the above steps until all the batter is finished, ensuring you put ½ tablespoon of olive oil into the pan each time.
7. Serve the gluten-free crepes with a sweet or savory filling of your choice.

Serves: 9 crepes

Nutritional Information:

Calories (Total): 1910kcal 87%. Carbohydrates: 160g 58%. Protein: 63g 58%. Fat: 100g 136%. Saturated Fat: 24g 97%. Cholesterol: 362mg 121%. Sodium:1055mg 70%. Fiber: 83g 332%. Sugar: 44g 80%. Vitamin A: 1598IU 32%. Vitamin C: 0.2mg 0%. Calcium: 667mg 67%. Iron: 1.7mg 9%. Potassium: 900mg 19%.

These banana muffins are ideal if you want a breakfast on the go. If you use extra large bananas, you may be able to make 11 or 12 muffins too.

Ingredients

½ cup coconut flour
1 teaspoon coconut oil, plus more for greasing
½ teaspoon baking soda
2 mashed ripe bananas
3 eggs
2-4 tablespoons of whole cane sugar, maple syrup or honey
1 teaspoon vanilla extract (optional)
½ teaspoon ground nutmeg
¼ teaspoon salt

Method

1. Preheat the oven to 350 degrees. Into a bowl, combine the ripe bananas, coconut oil, eggs, whole cane sugar and coconut flour, stirring until well blended. Add in the remaining ingredients: the baking soda, ground nutmeg and the salt until the mixture is smooth.
2. Prepare some paper muffin liners, using a little extra coconut oil to grease them with. Divide the batter so it's spread evenly between each muffin liner, of which there should be ten. The muffins should be about half full.
3. Bake in the oven at 350 degrees for around 23- 25 minutes, until the tops of the muffins are a golden brown color. Then leave to cool before serving.

Serves: 10

Nutritional Information:

Calories (Total): 1222kcal 56%. Carbohydrates: 142g 52%. Protein: 46g 42%. Fat: 36g 49%. Saturated Fat: 26g 107%. Cholesterol: 558mg 186%. Sodium: 818mg 55%. Fiber: 49g 195%. Sugar: 57g 103%. Vitamin A: 928IU 19%. Vitamin C: 21mg 28%. Calcium: 210mg 21%. Iron: 10.5mg 58%. Potassium: 1062mg 23%.

Breads

Coconut Flour Bread

This bread is a delicious and refreshing alternative to traditional breads made using wheat. The flavor is much the same and the coconut flour's flavor is not overpowering.

Ingredients

¾ cup of sifted organic coconut flour
4 tablespoons of sugar or a sweetener of your choice
½ cup melted butter
6 eggs
1 teaspoon baking powder
1 teaspoon vanilla extract
½ cup milk
½ teaspoon salt

Method

1. Into a bowl whisk the melted butter, eggs, vanilla extract, sugar and the salt together.
2. Combine the coconut flour along with the baking powder together, whisking thoroughly into the batter until there are no lumps remaining. Add in the milk.
3. Pour the mixture into a greased 9x5x3 loaf pan. Place in the oven and bake for 40 minutes at 350 degrees. Take this out of the pan and then cool on the rack.

Serves: 10-12

Nutritional Information:

Calories (Total): 2394kcal 109%. Carbohydrates: 181g 66%. Protein: 71g 65%. Fat: 157g 214%. Saturated Fat: 85g 349%. Cholesterol: 1264mg 421%. Sodium: 2594mg 173%. Fiber: 76g 303%. Sugar: 49g 89%. Vitamin A: 5001IU 100%. Vitamin C: 0.7mg 1%. Calcium: 634mg 63%. Iron: 7.3mg 41%. Potassium: 722mg 15%.

Coconut Flour Banana Bread

This tasty banana bread will soon become a firm staple in your baking collection once you taste the delicious flavors.

Ingredients

12 egg whites
1 cup banana puree
1 cup coconut flour
1 teaspoon homemade corn free baking powder
4 teaspoon vanilla extract
2 teaspoon saigon cinnamon
¼ teaspoon nutmeg
¾ cup water
½ teaspoon salt
6 droppers vanilla extract

Method

1. Beat the egg whites in a bowl until peaks begin to form.
2. Into a mixing bowl combine all of the above ingredients apart from the egg whites.
3. Return to the other bowl and continue beating the egg whites and fold into the mixture until well combined.
4. Pour the mixture into a greased bread pan and bake in the oven for 45 minutes to 1 hour, baking at 375 degrees.

Serves: 8

Nutritional Information:

Calories (Total): 2738kcal 124%. Carbohydrates: 158g 58%. Protein: 115g 104%. Fat: 126g 172%. Saturated Fat: 35g 144%. Cholesterol: 2028mg 676%. Sodium: 3824mg 255%.

Fiber: 83g 332%. Sugar: 118g 214%. Vitamin A: 3850IU 77%. Vitamin C: 1.5mg 2%. Calcium: 690mg 69%. Iron: 8.8mg 49%. Potassium: 1074mg 23%.

Coconut Flour Corn Bread

This corn bread is a healthy gluten-free version of the traditional one. It's also sweet and moist, with a subtle flavor of coconut that's not too overbearing.

Dry Ingredients

¼ cup sifted coconut flour
½ teaspoon baking powder
1/3 cup cornmeal
½ teaspoon salt

Wet Ingredients:

1/3 cup honey
1/3 cup melted butter
6 eggs
½ teaspoon vanilla

Method

1. Combine the dry ingredients, i.e. the sifted coconut flour, baking powder, cornmeal and the salt together into a mixing bowl. Sifted coconut flour is recommended for a finer texture. Separately blend together all of the wet ingredients: honey, melted butter, eggs and vanilla.
2. Combine the dry and wet ingredients together, whisking until there are no lumps.
3. Bake at 400 degrees for 15-18 minutes in the oven.

Serves: 2-4

Nutritional Information:

Calories (Total): 1600kcal 73%. Carbohydrates: 194g 70%. Protein: 56g 51%. Fat: 64g 87%. Saturated Fat: 23g 95%. Cholesterol: 1014mg 338%. Sodium: 2487mg 166%. Fiber: 29g 114%. Sugar: 103g 187%. Vitamin A: 1925IU 39%. Vitamin C: 1.3mg 2%. Calcium: 358mg 36%. Iron: 6.8mg 38%. Potassium: 567mg 12%.

It might sound like an odd combination, but bananas and avocados compliment each other well in this simple bread recipe. This is best served as a treat as it can be quite high in calories and (good) fats.

Ingredients

6 ripe bananas
3 ripe Haas avocados
½ cup coconut flour
4 cups rice flour
2½ cups whole sugar
½ cup melted coconut oil
1 tablespoon cinnamon
1 teaspoon ground cardamom
1 teaspoon powdered ginger
¾ teaspoon baking soda
1 ½ tablespoons baking powder
A pinch of salt

Method

1. Preheat the oven to 400 degrees F.
2. Into a food processor, mash the bananas and the avocados using a potato masher or a fork.
3. Add in the coconut flour, rice flour, whole sugar, coconut oil, cinnamon, ground cardamom, powdered ginger, baking soda, baking powder and the salt.
4. Combine all of these together using a mixer, whisk or a food processor.
5. Line 2 loaf pans using parchment paper. Evenly divide the thick mixture into the loaf pans.
6. Reduce the heat of the oven to 350 degrees and place the loaf pans into the oven. Bake this for 35-40

minutes, using a toothpick in the center of the mixture to ensure it comes out clean.

7. Lift the bread out of the pan, along the edges of the parchment. Leave to cool on the wire rack, before slicing and serving.

Serves: 12-14

Nutritional Information:

Calories (Total for 12-14 servings): 6687kcal 304%. Carbohydrates: 1294g 470%. Protein: 70g 64%. Fat: 155g 211%. Saturated Fat: 112g 457%. Cholesterol: 0mg 0%. Sodium: 1369mg 91%. Fiber: 95g 381%. Sugar: 667g 1213%. Vitamin A: 12IU 0%. Vitamin C: 109mg 146%. Calcium: 317mg 32%. Iron: 26mg 144%. Potassium: 4813mg 102%.

This is a quick and easy low-fat flat bread recipe that's perfect for creating sandwiches with when you're on the go...

Ingredients

1 egg
2 tablespoons liquid (coconut oil and/or water)
1 tablespoon coconut flour
A few crumbled herbs: basil, oregano, thyme and rosemary.
Cheese, one handful (optional)

Method

1. Heat the two tablespoons of liquid (coconut oil and/or water) in the skillet on a medium-low heat setting, mixing the egg, coconut flour and herbs into a bread batter. Allow this to slowly brown.
2. Once one side is done, you might want to melt cheese onto one half and flip it in the pan, doing the same on the other side.
3. Remove the bread from the heat and add on any other sandwich ingredients that you like.

Serves: 1-2

Nutritional Information:

Calories (Total): 343kcal 16%. Carbohydrates: 4.4g 2%. Protein: 7.3g 7%. Fat: 34g 46%. Saturated Fat: 5.9g 24%. Cholesterol: 186mg 62%. Sodium: 86mg 6%. Fiber: 2.5g 10%. Sugar: 1.1g 2%. Vitamin A: 270IU 5%. Vitamin C: 0mg 0%. Calcium: 28mg 3%. Iron: 0.9mg 5%. Potassium: 69mg 1%.

Chocolate Zucchini Bread

This is an unusual recipe that combines chocolate and zucchini to create a distinctive tasting bread – and it works. It's also perfect with a glass of coconut milk!

Ingredients

2 eggs, whisked
2 tablespoons coconut flour
1 teaspoon cinnamon
1 teaspoon vanilla extract
½ teaspoon baking soda
½ teaspoon baking powder
1 medium zucchini
¾ cup of SunButter or other nut butter
1/3 cup raw honey
A pinch of salt

Method

1. Preheat the oven to 375 degrees.
2. Shred the zucchini first, ideally using the shredding attachment on the food processor, or a cheese grater.
3. Once the zucchini has been shredded, remove any excess liquid using a couple of paper towels on the kitchen counter, and on top of the zucchini until it's been thoroughly squeezed. The idea is to make the zucchini feel waterless.
4. Place the zucchini and the other ingredients into a bowl. Using a large spoon, mix until all of the ingredients are combined well, creating a dark chocolate color.
5. Pour all of the ingredients into a loaf pan and place in the oven for around 25-35 minutes, until when tested with a toothpick, it will come out clean when poked. In some cases it may take the whole 35 minutes to cook.
6. Leave to cool before cutting and serving.

Serves: 4-6

Nutritional Information:

Calories (Total): 1589kcal 72%. Carbohydrates: 116g 42%. Protein: 53g 48%. Fat: 99g 134%. Saturated Fat: 14.7g 60%. Cholesterol: 372mg 124%. Sodium: 1372mg 91%. Fiber: 28g 112%. Sugar: 84g 153%. Vitamin A: 601IU 12%. Vitamin C: 3.9mg 5%. Calcium: 271mg 27%. Iron: 9.9mg 55%. Potassium: 205mg 4%.

This easy to make pumpkin bread makes an ideal breakfast or snack, especially when served with peanut butter or your favorite chocolate spread.

Dry Ingredients

¼ cup coconut flour
2 tablespoons cinnamon
½ teaspoon baking powder
½ teaspoon nutmeg
½ teaspoon ground cloves

Wet Ingredients

1 cup blanched almond oil
4 eggs
1 tablespoon coconut oil
1 cup pumpkin puree
1 teaspoon vanilla extract

Method

1. Mix all of the dry ingredients from the list above, then add in the beaten eggs along with the rest of the wet ingredients.
2. Grease the baking pan with a little coconut oil to ensure the batter doesn't stick, then place the mixture into a loaf pan.
3. Bake at 375 degrees for about 40 minutes before taking out of the oven. Leave to cool before serving.

Serves: 4

Nutritional Information:

Calories (Total): 2731kcal 124%. Carbohydrates: 67g 24%. Protein: 38g 35%. Fat: 259g 354%. Saturated Fat: 28g 114%. Cholesterol: 744mg 248%. Sodium: 583mg 39%. Fiber: 39g 154%. Sugar: 15.6g 28%. Vitamin A: 31,127+IU 623%. Vitamin C: 3.8mg 5%. Calcium: 378mg 38%. Iron: 6.1mg 34%. Potassium: 356mg 8%.

Lunches

Coconut Flour Cheese Crackers

These cheese crackers make for a tasty snack at lunch, either on their own or as a compliment to a sandwich.

Ingredients

1 organic egg
½ cup coconut flour
2 tablespoons grass-fed butter
1½ cups shredded cheddar cheese
A pinch of salt

Method

1. Preheat the oven to 400 degrees F.
2. Use a high-powered food blender or a food processor to create the cracker batter by blending the egg, coconut flour, grass-fed butter and cheddar cheese and salt together until the ingredients are well combined.
3. Onto a piece of parchment paper or a lined cookie sheet, spread the cracker batter. Place another piece of the parchment paper on top of the mixture and use a rolling pin to spread the batter thinly. Gently pull off the parchment paper.
4. Bake the crackers in the oven for 10 minutes. Take out of the oven and score with either a knife or a pizza cutter. Return the crackers to the oven and bake continuously until the crackers are light brown and crispy, which should take 5-10 minutes.

Serves: 32 crackers

Nutritional Information:

Calories (Total): 1369kcal 62%. Carbohydrates: 70g 25%. Protein: 65g 59%. Fat: 84g 115%. Saturated Fat: 48g 196%. Cholesterol: 364mg 121%. Sodium: 1381mg 92%. Fiber: 42g 166%. Sugar: 9.8g 18%. Vitamin A: 1968IU 39%. Vitamin C: 0mg 0%. Calcium: 1250mg 125%. Iron: 2.1mg 12%. Potassium: 235mg 5%.

Coconut Flour Sweet Potato Soup

This soup is full of nutrients and super easy to make too. If you don't like dairy, you can use almond, coconut or rice milk to make it dairy-free instead.

Ingredients
1 tablespoon virgin coconut oil
1 tablespoon coconut flour
1 ½ cups chicken or vegetable broth
1 ½ cups cooked cubed sweet potatoes
¼ teaspoon ground or fresh ginger
1/8 teaspoon ground nutmeg
1/8 teaspoon ground cinnamon
1 cup milk
Salt and pepper (to taste)

Method
1. Into a heavy saucepan placed over a medium-low heat, cook the virgin coconut oil and the coconut flour together, stirring constantly until it turns a lightish caramel color. Add in the chicken broth and then bring to the boil, before lowering to a simmer.
2. Stir in the sweet potatoes as well as the spices. Bring to a simmer once more and then cook the soup for an extra 5 minutes.
3. Puree the soup into a blender in batches. Return to the saucepan and then add the cup of milk, while gently reheating the soup. Add any more seasonings as necessary and then add salt and pepper before serving.

Serves: 4

Nutritional Information:

Calories (Total): 634kcal 29%. Carbohydrates: 92g 33%. Protein: 24g 22%. Fat: 17.8g 24%. Saturated Fat: 14.3g 59%. Cholesterol: 4.9mg 2%. Sodium: 1397mg 93%. Fiber: 12.6g 50%. Sugar: 33g 61%. Vitamin A: 57,672+IU 1153%. Vitamin C: 61mg 82%. Calcium: 433mg 43%. Iron: 3mg 17%. Potassium: 2143mg 46%.

If you're looking to make wheat-free bagels, these should satisfy your craving.

Ingredients

½ cup sifted coconut flour
1/3 cups butter, melted
6 eggs
1½ teaspoons garlic powder
½ teaspoon baking powder
½ teaspoon salt
2 teaspoons guar or xanthan gum (optional)

Method

1. Blend the eggs, butter, garlic powder and the salt together.
2. Combine the baking powder with the coconut flour into a medium sized bowl, along with the guar or xanthan gum if you are using.
3. Whisk in the coconut flour mixture with the eggs mixture so that it forms a batter, ensuring there are no lumps. Spoon this into a greased donut pan and then bake for 15 minutes at 400 degrees F.
4. Leave to cool for a couple of minutes and then serve and enjoy!

Serves: 6 bagels

Nutritional Information:

Calories (Total): 1260kcal 57%. Carbohydrates: 81g 30%. Protein: 55g 50%. Fat: 71g 97%. Saturated Fat: 32g 130%.

Cholesterol: 1116mg 372%. Sodium: 862mg 57%. Fiber: 48g 192%. Sugar: 12.9g 23%. Vitamin A: 1620+IU 32%. Vitamin C: 0.8mg 1%. Calcium: 251mg 25%. Iron: 5.6mg 31%. Potassium: 460mg 10%.

These doughy pretzels make for an excellent paleo version of an all-time American classic and are especially delicious when served with mustard.

Ingredients

1 cup coconut flour
½ cup tapioca flour
½ teaspoons baking soda
½ teaspoons baking powder
2 tablespoons of apple cider vinegar
1 egg
2 tablespoons melted butter
½ cup butter, Olive Oil or Ghee
½ cup of water
½ teaspoon of sea salt
1 tablespoon of coarse salt

Method

1. Over a medium heat place a small pan and add in the butter, water, sea salt and the vinegar, bringing to the boil. Remove the pan from off the heat and place on a counter top.
2. Add the tapioca flour and for 2 minutes, stir until it forms a wet paste.
3. Add in the baking powder and soda, stirring until the mixture starts to foam – this should take around 3 seconds.
4. Place the dough onto a piece of parchment paper and knead for around 30 seconds to 1 minute. If it's troublesome to combine, place it in a food processor or use the Blendtec/Vitamix to get it to form a dough.
5. Pinch a 1" – 2" piece of the dough and roll it until it's ½" round by 6"-7" long. Keep twisting the dough until it

forms a pretzel shape and place on the parchment paper on a baking sheet, brushing with the butter.
6. Sprinkle some coarse salt onto the surface and bake in the oven for 25-30 minutes at 350 degrees F.

Serves: 10

Nutritional Information:

Calories (Total): 2320kcal 105%. Carbohydrates: 194g 71%. Protein: 40g 36%. Fat: 144g 197%. Saturated Fat: 33g 133%. Cholesterol: 186mg 62%. Sodium: 8711mg 581%. Fiber: 83g 332%. Sugar: 17.1g 31%. Vitamin A: 270IU 5%. Vitamin C: 0mg 0%. Calcium: 188mg 19%. Iron: 0.9mg 5%. Potassium: 69mg 1%.

Coconut Flour Paleo Wraps

These coconut flour wraps are easy to make, incredibly versatile and taste delicious when filled with your favorite vegetable, fish or meat.

Ingredients

8 eggs
4 teaspoon coconut oil, melted
1 cup arrowroot flour
4 tablespoons coconut flour
½ teaspoon baking soda
A pinch of salt

Method

1. Whisk the eggs and the coconut oil together into a medium sized bowl.
2. Add in half a cup of the arrowroot flour into the eggs mixture and whisk until it's fully incorporated. This might be lumpy at first but keep whisking it until it's fully mixed in.
3. Add in the coconut flour, salt and the baking soda, whisking to ensure that the batter becomes smooth and lump-free.
4. Take a small frying pan and place over a medium heat. Add about a ¼ cup of the batter, allowing it to swirl around the pan in a thin layer. Cook this for around a minute and then start to peel it off the pan, using a spatula. Flip this over and cook for another minute on the other side.
5. Take the pan off the heat and allow it to cool for a few minutes on a cooling rack.
6. Store the wraps in a container, keeping them covered and in the refrigerator. The coconut flour wraps will last

for around one week, but they may need to be reheated for 20 seconds or so before using them.

Serves: 10

Nutritional Information:

Calories (Total): 1319kcal 60%. Carbohydrates: 134g 49%. Protein: 55g 50%. Fat: 59g 81%. Saturated Fat: 31g 125%. Cholesterol: 1488mg 496%. Sodium: 792mg 53%. Fiber: 14.4g 58%. Sugar: 6.8g 12%. Vitamin A: 2160IU 43%. Vitamin C: 0mg 0%. Calcium: 355mg 36%. Iron: 7.4mg 41%. Potassium: 567mg 12%.

This Italian flatbread recipe can be made low-carb and gluten-free. It also makes a delicious alternative to wheat free Panini breads and baguettes.

Ingredients

6 tablespoons coconut flour
3¼ cups almond flour
1/3 cup unflavored whey protein powder
¼ cup olive oil
¼ cup water
4 large eggs
½ teaspoon garlic powder
2 teaspoons baking powder

Method

1. Preheat the oven to 325F. Into a large bowl add the coconut flour, almond flour, whey protein powder, baking powder, salt and garlic, whisking them together. Whisk in the olive oil and eggs with the water until it's well combined. The dough should be relatively sticky at this point.
2. Cut a large piece of parchment paper and place it in a rough rectangle on top of the batter. Top this with another parchment piece.
3. Roll the flour mixture into a ½ inch by ¾ inch thick rectangle and place onto the large baking sheet, removing the top layer of the parchment.
4. Bake for another 20 minutes or so until the dough becomes firm to the touch.
5. Remove from out of the oven and leave it to cool completely before cutting it.

6. Use a bread knife to cut it into 10 sections. Each of the sections should be cut carefully so that the bready center is in two halves, before being filled with some of your favorite sandwich fillings.

Serves: 10

Nutritional Information:

Calories (Total): 3608kcal 164%. Carbohydrates: 109 g 40%. Protein: 85g 77%. Fat: 279g 380%. Saturated Fat: 31g 128%. Cholesterol: 871mg 290%. Sodium: 1318mg 88%. Fiber: 54g 216%. Sugar: 26g 48%. Vitamin A: 1080IU 22%. Vitamin C: 0.1mg 0%. Calcium: 1726mg 173%. Iron: 19.3mg 107%. Potassium: 725mg 15%.

This tastes great when made fresh than its store bought variety and can be made low fat by using dairy free cheese such as Daiya if required.

Ingredients

For the crust:
½ cup coconut flour
1 cup almond meal flour
1 tablespoon parsley, finely chopped
½ teaspoon sea salt
¼ cup liquified coconut oil
1 tablespoon water

For the filling:
4 whisked eggs
¼ cup finely chopped sundried tomatoes
1 cup sausage
1 onion
1 garlic clove
½ cup of fresh broccoli
4oz cheese (or Daiya or dairy-free cheese)
½ teaspoon sea salt

Method

Creating the Crust

1. Combine all of the crust ingredients together, blending well. Press the mixture using your hands into a deep pie pan.
2. Bake in the oven for 10 minutes at 350 degrees F and then leave to cool.

For the Filling

1. Sauté a small medium sized onion, finely chopped in a pan for about 10 minutes.
2. Add 1 clove of freshly minced garlic. Sauté this for a few minutes more, making sure not to burn.
3. Steam 2 cups of fresh broccoli that's been sliced into small bits, for around 5 minutes.
4. Add the garlic, onions and broccoli into a bowl along with the 4 whisked eggs, sausage, chopped sundried tomatoes, dairy-free cheese and the sea salt. Make sure to combine well.
5. Add the filling into the cooled crust. Bake in the oven for 30 minutes at 350 degrees F.

Serves: 2-4

Nutritional Information:

Calories (Total): 3370kcal 153%. Carbohydrates: 132g 48%. Protein: 147g 134%. Fat: 253g 345%. Saturated Fat: 121g 493%. Cholesterol: 998mg 333%. Sodium: 5786mg 386%. Fiber: 67g 270%. Sugar: 15.8g 29%. Vitamin A: 3937U 79%. Vitamin C: 63mg 84%. Calcium: 1351mg 135%. Iron: 14mg 78%. Potassium: 1838mg 39%.

Dinners

Coconut Flour Pizza Crust

This is a relatively low fat pizza crust that makes for a simple and healthy meal, especially when you add your own choice of fresh toppings.

Ingredients
2 tablespoons coconut flour
2 tablespoons plain yogurt
2 eggs
½ teaspoon onion powder
½ teaspoon oregano
½ teaspoon basil
½ teaspoon garlic
4 tablespoons parmesan cheese
Salt to taste

Method

1. Mix the coconut flour, eggs and the yogurt together until no lumps remain. Add in the parmesan cheese and the spices to the mixture. The batter will be thin at first but will eventually come together.
2. Pour the batter onto a piece of parchment paper that is 5 inches round. Try to get the batter as evenly distributed as is possible.
3. Place in the oven and bake for 15 minutes at 375 degrees. After being taken out of the oven, pour on your own tomato sauce and cheese, adding on your favorite vegetable toppings such as zucchini, spinach, mushrooms and tomatoes as required.

Serves: 1

Nutritional Information:

Calories (Total): 316kcal 14%. Carbohydrates: 14.6g 5%. Protein: 24g 22%. Fat: 16.6g 23%. Saturated Fat: 7.2g 29%. Cholesterol: 386mg 129%. Sodium: 536mg 36%. Fiber: 5.6g 22%. Sugar: 5.4g 10%. Vitamin A: 668IU 13%. Vitamin C: 0.5mg 1%. Calcium: 385mg 39%. Iron: 2mg 11%. Potassium: 267mg 6%.

Coconut flour tortillas are excellent served with your favorite meats and vegetables and are perfect for either lunch or dinner.

Ingredients

¼ cup coconut flour
¼ teaspoon baking powder
½ teaspoon chile powder
8 large egg whites
½ cup water
1 tablespoon of butter or coconut oil for frying

Method

1. Whisk all of the above ingredients into a large bowl and blend until it forms a smooth batter.
2. Preheat an 8" nonstick skillet and place over a medium heat. Place 1 teaspoon of oil or butter into the pan, swirling to ensure that it's coated evenly.
3. Ladle 2-3 tablespoons of the batter into pan, tipping it from side to side so that a thin layer of batter forms across the entire surface.
4. Once the first side is golden brown, take a thin spatula and flip over to the other side during the cooking process – do this until it's golden brown.
5. Take the tortilla and place onto a wire rack, repeating the process from the beginning using the butter or oil. This will make 8 tortillas.

Serves: 8

Nutritional Information:

Calories (Total): 1222kcal 56%. Carbohydrates: 46g 17%. Protein: 59g 53%. Fat: 83g 113%. Saturated Fat: 38g 155%. Cholesterol: 1488mg 496%. Sodium: 2487mg 166%. Fiber: 21g 83%. Sugar: 8.9g 16%. Vitamin A: 2160IU 43%. Vitamin C: 0mg 0%. Calcium: 264mg 26%. Iron: 7mg 39%. Potassium: 552mg 12%.

Coconut Chickpea Stew

This stew uses coconut flour to add substantial thickness to the spicy and aromatic flavors of the garam masala powder and the coconut milk.

Ingredients

2 tablespoons coconut oil
2 tablespoons coconut flour
1 serrano pepper, diced
1 big onion, diced
3 garlic cloves, diced
2 tablespoons minced ginger
2 cans of garbanzo beans
1 can tomatoes with onions
1 can lite coconut milk
1.5 tablespoons garam masala powder
½ cup cilantro
Rice (if desired)

Method
1. Sautee the garlic, onion and the ginger into a pan with the coconut oil on a medium high heat. Brown for 6-8 minutes before adding to a crockpot, along with the other ingredients.
2. Cover the pot and cook for 4-6 hours on a low setting.
3. Once ready, serve the coconut chickpea stew over rice and garnish with a little cilantro.

Serves: 2-3

Nutritional Information:

Calories (Total): 1111kcal 51%. Carbohydrates: 106g 39%. Protein: 33g 30%. Fat: 66g 90%. Saturated Fat: 42g 155%. Cholesterol: 0mg 0%. Sodium: 2180mg 145%. Fiber: 24g 95%. Sugar: 27g 50%. Vitamin A: 2021IU 40%. Vitamin C: 47mg 62%. Calcium: 425mg 43%. Iron: 6mg 33%. Potassium: 1006mg 21%.

Paleo Tuna Spinach Casserole

This makes a filling meal, protein rich and satisfying it will fill you up and provide with a wide range of vitamins and minerals.

Ingredients

2 cups baby spinach
2 small cans of drained tuna
1 chopped onion
2 eggs, slightly beaten
1/3 cup coconut milk
1 tablespoon coconut flour
1 tablespoon dried parsley
1 tablespoon garlic powder
½ cup dairy free cheese substitute
½ cup of sliced almonds
A few sprays of cooking oil

Method

1. Preheat the oven to 375 degrees F and take a 9 inch casserole dish, spraying it with a little cooking oil.
2. Into a large bowl stir all of the above ingredients, except for the cheese and cooking spray.
3. Transfer the mixture into a casserole dish and sprinkle the cheese on top.
4. Bake in the oven for 35-50 minutes. Leave to cool for a few minutes and then serve, sprinkling a little unsweetened shredded coconut onto the top if desired.

Serves: 2

Nutritional Information:

Calories (Total): 1137kcal 52%. Carbohydrates: 46g 17%. Protein: 116g 105%. Fat: 52g 71%. Saturated Fat: 11.7g 48%. Cholesterol: 471mg 157%. Sodium: 943mg 63%. Fiber:14.9g 60%. Sugar: 10.7g 19%. Vitamin A: 6769IU 135%. Vitamin C: 29mg 39%. Calcium: 441mg 44%. Iron: 11.5mg 64%. Potassium: 1488mg 32%.

This coconut chicken dish uses flaked coconut not flour – but is an excellent example of how other coconut derivatives can be used to flavor meats such as chicken.

Ingredients

Coconut Chicken:

4 ounces boneless and skinless chicken breasts
2 eggs, lightly beaten
1/3 cup melted butter
¾ cup flaked coconut
¾ cup crushed corn flakes
¼ teaspoon garlic powder
½ teaspoon salt
¼ teaspoon black pepper
Cooking spray

Plum Sauce:
3 cups light bodied red wine
1 cup dried plum
1/3 cup sugar
2 tablespoons red wine vinegar

Method

1. Preheat the oven to 400 degrees F. Into a shallow dish, add the flaked coconut, salt, pepper, garlic powder and the corn flakes crumbs, mixing to combine. Into another shallow dish, lightly beat two eggs. Prepare a shallow baking pan and spray it lightly with cooking spray.

2. Dip each of the chicken breasts into the coconut and egg mixture, coating all areas of the chicken breast. Place each of the pieces on the baking dish and add in the drizzled melted butter, baking for 25-30 minutes. After this time, take an internal probe thermometer and place inside of the chicken, ensuring that the chicken has reached 165 degrees once cooked.

3. Prepare the plum sauce as the chicken is cooking. Combine the plum sauce ingredients listed above, into a large saucepan. Bring to a simmer over a medium heat. Leave this to simmer for 20 minutes until the plums start to soften. Leave this to cool slightly and then add the plums into a food processor, so the mixture can be pureed. Serve with the coconut chicken.

Serves: 4

Nutritional Information:

Calories (Total): 2823kcal 128%. Carbohydrates: 346g 126%. Protein: 45g 41%. Fat: 90g 122%. Saturated Fat: 58g 235%. Cholesterol: 437mg 146%. Sodium: 1080mg 72%. Fiber:52g 209%. Sugar: 207g 376%. Vitamin A: 3688IU 74%. Vitamin C: 4.8mg 6%. Calcium: 169mg 17%. Iron: 14.9mg 83%. Potassium: 1800mg 38%.

Coconut Flour Meatloaf

This meatloaf is best served with thick gravy, potatoes and roasted vegetables.

Ingredients

2 tablespoons coconut flour
1 egg
1 tablespoon raw apple cider vinegar or coconut water vinegar
1 tablespoon agave nectar
1 pound grass-fed ground beef
1 clove garlic, minced
¼ of a large onion
5 baby carrots, chopped
1 celery stalk, chopped
1 clove minced garlic
8oz organic tomato sauce
½ teaspoon basil
½ teaspoon oregano
¼ teaspoon ground black pepper
1 teaspoon salt

Method

1. Into a large bowl, beat an egg slightly.
2. Add all of the rest of the ingredients, apart from the ground beef. Stir everything together until it's well combined.
3. Incorporate the ground beef into the mixture and form into a loaf shape in the middle of a 9x13 pan.
4. Bake in the oven for 35 minutes at 350 degrees F.

Serves: 2

Nutritional Information:

Calories (Total): 684kcal 31%. Carbohydrates: 47g 17%. Protein: 51g 46%. Fat: 30g 40%. Saturated Fat: 10.9g 45%. Cholesterol: 320mg 107%. Sodium: 1839mg 123%. Fiber:12.9g 52%. Sugar: 26g 47%. Vitamin A: 7838IU 157%. Vitamin C: 11.1mg 15%. Calcium: 81mg 8%. Iron: 5.9mg 33%. Potassium: 1368mg 29%.

This pie crust is easy to prepare and can be made savory or sweet, depending on your choice of toppings.

Ingredients

¾ cup coconut flour
2 eggs
½ cup grass fed butter
1-3 tablespoons raw honey
¼ teaspoon sea salt

Method

1. Preheat the oven to 400 degrees. Mix the eggs, butter, honey and the sea salt together into a medium sized bowl. Add in the coconut flour, stirring until the dough is holding firmly together.
2. Gather the dough into a ball shape, patting it down into a 9" greased pie pan. Prick the dough with a fork before baking it for 9 minutes. Leave it to cool before serving.

Serves: 2-4

Nutritional Information:

Calories (Total): 1397kcal 64%. Carbohydrates: 120g 44%. Protein: 37g 34%. Fat: 74g 100%. Saturated Fat: 36g 149%. Cholesterol: 370mg 123%. Sodium: 703mg 47%. Fiber: 62g 249%. Sugar: 30g 55%. Vitamin A: 485IU 10%. Vitamin C: 0mg 0%. Calcium: 53mg 5%. Iron: 1.8mg 10%. Potassium: 133mg 3%.

Desserts

Chocolate and Coconut Flour Cake

This chocolate coconut flour cake tastes delicious and the below recipe will fit in two 5 inch cake pans.

Ingredients
½ cup coconut oil (or ghee)
¾ cup maple syrup
½ cup brewed coffee
1 tablespoon vanilla extract
2/3 cup coconut flour
½ cup high quality cacao powder
½ teaspoon baking soda
6 eggs
Parchment paper for lining the cake pans

Method

1. Preheat the oven to 350 degrees F.
2. After greasing the cake pans, line the bottoms with the parchment paper.
3. Combine the cacao powder, baking soda, coconut flour and the salt into a small bowl and then set to the side.
4. Whisk the eggs in a bowl and then add in the butter/ghee or coconut oil, ½ cup of coffee, ¾ cup of maple syrup and the vanilla extract until the mixture is well combined.
5. Add the dry ingredients (coconut flour, cacao powder, baking soda) and mix well with the wet ingredients.
6. Mix on a low speed until all of the dry ingredients are completely combined, which should take about 30 seconds.

7. Scrape the sides of the mixing bowl, beating the cake batter on a high speed for one minute or so until fluffy.
8. Divide the batter between the two pans, spreading evenly.
9. Bake in the oven for 25-30 minutes, until when a toothpick is fully inserted, it comes out clean.
10. Leave to cool on a wire rack for about 10-15 minutes. Loosen the sides of the cake from the pan using a knife, then turn it out onto the wire rack and leave to cool completely.

Serves: 2-4

Nutritional Information:

Calories (Total): 1554kcal 71%. Carbohydrates: 208g 76%. Protein: 71g 64%. Fat: 82g 111%. Saturated Fat: 47g 192%. Cholesterol: 1116mg 372%. Sodium: 848mg 57%. Fiber: 51g 205%. Sugar: 111g 201%. Vitamin A: 1461IU 29%. Vitamin C: 0mg 0%. Calcium: 442mg 44%. Iron: 22mg 122%. Potassium: 789mg 17%.

Coconut Flour Shortbread Cookies

These are super easy to make and only involve 3-4 ingredients!

Ingredients

3 tablespoons coconut flour
2 tablespoons organic butter or coconut oil
1 tablespoon honey
Lemon, orange zest, vanilla or cinnamon (Optional for flavor variations)

Method

1. Mix the coconut flour, organic butter/oil, honey and lemon zest together until they're well combined and forming a thick paste.
2. Shape into a ball and press down gently using a fork or your hand. This will ensure that the cookies won't spread while baking.
3. Place in the oven for 8-10 minutes at 350F until they just begin to brown on the bottom.
4. Be careful not to get them out of the pan too soon, as they may crumble!

Serves: 4-5

Nutritional Information:

Calories (Total): 353kcal 16%. Carbohydrates: 29g 11%. Protein:3g 3%. Fat: 24g 33%. Saturated Fat: 16.8g 69%. Cholesterol: 60mg 20%. Sodium: 195mg 13%. Fiber: 7.5g 30%. Sugar: 17.5g 32%. Vitamin A: 0IU 0%. Vitamin C: 0mg 0%. Calcium: 0mg 0%. Iron: 0mg 0%. Potassium: 0mg 0%.

Coconut Flour Zucchini Brownies

These zucchini brownies make for a sweet treat and will be a firm favorite with the whole family!

Ingredients

1 cup coconut flour
¾ cup cocoa powder
½ cup shredded zucchini
1/3 cup applesauce
2 teaspoons pure vanilla extract
1 cup plus 2 tablespoons water
3 tablespoons flaxmeal
½ cup plus 2 tablespoons vegetable or coconut oil
½ teaspoon baking soda
¾ cup xylitol or a sugar/sweetener of your choice
1/16 teaspoon pure stevia extract, or 2 tablespoons sugar
½ cup mini chocolate chips (optional)

Method

1. Preheat the oven to 350F and taking a 9x13" baking dish, line it with parchment paper and set aside.
2. Into a large mixing bowl, whisk together the shredded zucchini, applesauce, cup of water, 2 teaspoons of pure vanilla extract, 3 tablespoons of flaxmeal and the ½ cup of vegetable or coconut oil, leaving to sit for at least 5 minutes.
3. Combine all of the rest of the ingredients into a separate bowl, stirring well. Pour the wet ingredients into the dry, stirring until it's all evenly mixed and then pour into the baking dish.
4. Use a full sheet of either wax or parchment paper, pressing down very firmly until the brownie batter

completely covers the pan. Bake this in the oven for 19-20 minutes, patting it down hard with either a pancake spatula or a sheet of parchment paper.
5. Leave the zucchini brownies to sit for 15 minutes before cutting them into squares. Cutting them with a plastic knife is best to prevent crumbling.

Serves: 20-24 squares

Nutritional Information:

Calories (Total): 2294kcal 104%. Carbohydrates: 350g 127%. Protein: 65g 59%. Fat: 97g 132%. Saturated Fat: 38g 153%. Cholesterol: 0mg 0%. Sodium: 910mg 61%. Fiber: 115g 461%. Sugar: 136g 248%. Vitamin A: 124IU 2%. Vitamin C: 10.9mg 15%. Calcium: 123mg 12%. Iron: 11.9mg 66%. Potassium: 1271mg 27%.

Red Velvet Coconut Flour Cupcakes

These can make a healthy dessert alternative, while being both light and sweet with a smooth, buttery flavor.

Ingredients

Dry Ingredients
2 tablespoons unsweetened cocoa powder
½ cup coconut flour
¼ teaspoon baking soda
¼ teaspoon sea salt

Wet Ingredients
4 large eggs
½ cup agave nectar
2 tablespoons grapeseed oil
1 tablespoon food coloring, made from vegetable dye

Cream Cheese Frosting:

8 ounces cream cheese (at room temperature)
¾ cup heavy cream
¼ cup agave nectar

Method

1. Preheat the oven to 350 degrees F and line 9 muffin cups with paper liners.
2. Combine all of the dry ingredients into a bowl and make sure you sift in the coconut flour.
3. Whisk all the wet ingredients into a medium sized bowl. Then blend the dry and wet ingredients together with a handheld mixer.

4. Scoop ¼ cup of batter into the muffin cup and bake for 18-22 minutes until once a toothpick is inserted, it can come out clean.
5. Leave it to cool for one hour, frost and then serve.
6. Make the cream cheese frosting in the meantime, whipping the heavy cream into a mixer so that it creates stiff peak forms. Into a separate bowl, whip the agave nectar and cream cheese until well combined.
7. Fold in the cream cheese mixture gently with the whipped cream, by using a rubber spatula. Add onto the cupcakes and serve.

The cream cheese and whipped cream mixture can be stored in a glass jar and kept for up to 2 days in the refrigerator.

Serves: 9 muffins

Nutritional Information:

Calories (Total): 2717kcal 124%. Carbohydrates: 214g 78%. Protein: 59g 53%. Fat: 165g 225%. Saturated Fat: 109g 448%. Cholesterol: 485mg 162%. Sodium: 1593mg 106%. Fiber: 54g 214%. Sugar: 136g 248%. Vitamin A: 5406IU 108%. Vitamin C: 0mg 0%. Calcium: 204mg 20%. Iron: 10.3mg 57%. Potassium: 649mg 14%.

Coconut Flour Strawberry Shortcake

Strawberries and cream are the perfect compliment to this shortcake, making it taste fresh and delicious.

Ingredients
½ cup coconut flour
2 cups organic almond flour
½ cup shredded coconut
2 tablespoons baking powder
1 cup milk
1 egg
1 tablespoon organic whole sugar
1 teaspoon salt
½ cup coconut oil

Toppings:
1 teaspoon vanilla extract
Organic whole sugar
1 cup heavy cream
Fresh strawberries or any type of flavored fruit

Method

1. Mix all of the dry ingredients: the coconut flour, almond flour, shredded coconut, baking powder, sugar and salt into a bowl.
2. Set the bowl aside and add the wet ingredients, i.e. the milk, coconut oil and the egg, combining together until the dough becomes finely textured. The ingredients need to be mixed together smoothly, but not so much that the cake's texture is overdone.
3. Flatten the dough until it's of about 2 inches of thickness before being cut. Cooking time should ideally

take 10-12 minutes when placed in the oven at 450 degrees.
4. Whip the heavy cream, organic whole sugar and vanilla extract together in a bowl to create the creamy topping.
5. Once the base of the cake is cooked, set it aside and leave it to cool before adding the cream and the strawberries.

Serves: 2-4

Nutritional Information:

Calories (Total): 4335kcal 197%. Carbohydrates: 356g 129%. Protein: 69g 63%. Fat: 303g 413%. Saturated Fat: 236g 966%. Cholesterol: 532mg 177%. Sodium: 1253mg 84%. Fiber:102g 408%. Sugar: 63g 115%. Vitamin A: 3815IU 76%. Vitamin C: 91mg 121%. Calcium: 754mg 75%. Iron: 12.6mg 70%. Potassium: 627mg 13%.

Coconut Pineapple Cake

This coconut and pineapple cake is bursting with exotic flavors that are sure to tantalize your tongue.

Ingredients

2 cups sugar
2 cups coconut flour
½ teaspoon baking powder
1 teaspoon vanilla extract
2 eggs
½ teaspoon baking soda
1 can crushed pineapple, undrained
½ cup chopped walnuts
½ teaspoon salt

Frosting
½ cup flaked coconut
2 cups confectioners' sugar
½ cup softened butter
1 package of softened cream cheese

Method

1. Beat the eggs, vanilla and the sugar together in a bowl until fluffy. Alternate with combining these ingredients: the baking soda, baking powder, coconut flour, salt and the egg mixture with the pineapple. Then stir in the walnuts.
2. Pour the mixture into a 13" x 9" inch greased baking pan and bake in the oven for 35-40 minutes at 350 degrees F. Insert a toothpick and if it comes out clean, it's ready. Leave to cool on a wire rack.
3. Into the small bowl add the cream cheese, confectioners' sugar and the butter together until it

creates a smooth frosting. Frost the cake and then sprinkle on the flaked coconut before storing in the refrigerator.

Serves: 12

Nutritional Information:

Calories (Total): 7146kcal 325%. Carbohydrates: 1197g 435%. Protein: 99g 90%. Fat: 204g 278%. Saturated Fat: 105g 430%. Cholesterol: 94mg 31%. Sodium: 2434mg 162%. Fiber:180g 720%. Sugar: 587g 1067%. Vitamin A: 1239IU 25%. Vitamin C: 24mg 32%. Calcium: 709mg 71%. Iron: 84mg 465%. Potassium: 519mg 11%.

Coconut Flour Carrot Cake

This carrot cake is completely grain-free and makes the perfect accompaniment when served with afternoon tea or coffee.

Ingredients

¾ cup coconut flour sifted
1½ tablespoons ground organic saigon cinnamon
1 teaspoon baking soda
5 carrots, peeled and shredded
1 cup maple syrup
1 teaspoon organic nutmeg
1 teaspoon sea salt
1 tablespoon pure vanilla extract
1 cup organic coconut oil
10 eggs, pastured
1 tablespoon pure vanilla extract
1 ¾ cup raw pumpkin puree

Cream Cheese Frosting
1 tablespoon pure vanilla extract
16oz full fat cream cheese
1 ½ tablespoons grated ginger root
½ cup organic maple syrup

Method

1. Preheat the oven to 325 degrees F.
2. Begin by marinating the carrots in maple syrup in a medium sized saucepan, before refrigerating for an hour.
3. Into a mixing bowl sift the coconut flour, cinnamon, nutmeg, baking soda and the sea salt. Mix in 1 tablespoon of maple syrup with the pumpkin puree.

4. Into a large bowl, add the coconut oil, eggs, pure vanilla extract and the pumpkin puree mixture. Combine the wet and the dry ingredients, folding into the mixture using a plastic spatula.
5. Stir in the marinated carrots with the cake batter.
6. Using two 9-inch cake pans (or one large cake pan), grease with coconut oil or use parchment paper to line the pans, for ease of removal.
7. Bake in the oven for 35 minutes. Test the center of the cake by taking a toothpick and if it comes out clean, the cakes are ready.
8. Remove the cakes from out of the oven and leave to cool before frosting.
9. Use a hand or kitchen mixer to blend the ingredients for the cream cheese frosting: softened cream cheese, ginger, vanilla and the maple syrup together. Use immediately on the cakes or refrigerate and save for later.

Serves: 12

Nutritional Information:

Calories (Total): 5705kcal 259%. Carbohydrates: 518g 188%. Protein: 94g 86%. Fat: 362g 494%. Saturated Fat: 270g 1106%. Cholesterol: 0mg 0%. Sodium: 3521mg 235%. Fiber:93g 373%. Sugar: 382g 695%. Vitamin A: 55,536+IU 1111%. Vitamin C: 37mg 49%. Calcium: 641mg 64%. Iron: 22mg 122%. Potassium: 1792mg 38%.

Thank you for reading this recipe book and I hope it will help you to make delicious coconut flour recipes.

If you enjoyed *35 Coconut Flour Recipes…*I would appreciate if you could leave a review on Amazon to let others know if this was helpful.

21735605R00043

Printed in Great Britain
by Amazon